BOUND FOR AMERICA

The Forced Migration of Africans to the New World

James Haskins & Kathleen Benson

PAINTINGS BY Floyd Cooper

LOTHROP, LEE & SHEPARD BOOKS ❖ MORROW

New York

To Margaret Emily
—JH & KB
For my sons, Dayton and Kai
—FC

The authors are grateful to Barbara Ball Buff and
their tireless editor, Susan Pearson, for their help.

Oil wash on board was used for the full-color illustrations.
The text type is 13-point Sabon.

Published by Lothrop, Lee & Shepard Books
an imprint of Morrow Junior Books
a division of William Morrow and Company, Inc.
1350 Avenue of the Americas, New York, NY 10019
www.williammorrow.com

Printed in Singapore at Tien Wah Press.

10 9 8 7 6 5 4 3 2 1

Library of Congress Cataloging-in-Publication Data
Haskins, James, date.
Bound for America: the forced migration of Africans to the New World/
James Haskins & Kathleen Benson; paintings by Floyd Cooper.
p. cm.
Includes bibliographical references and index.
Summary: Discusses the European enslavement of Africans, including their capture,
branding, conditions on slave ships, shipboard mutinies, and arrival in the Americas.
ISBN 0-688-10258-1 (trade)—ISBN 0-688-10259-X (library)
1. Slave-trade—America—History—Juvenile literature.   2. Slave-trade—Africa—History—Juvenile literature.
3. Slavery—America—History—Juvenile literature.   [1. Slave trade—History.   2. Slavery—History.]
I. Benson, Kathleen.   II. Cooper, Floyd, ill.   III. Title.   HT1049.H37 1999
382'.44—dc21   98-24101   CIP   AC

Permission for photographs and illustrations is gratefully acknowledged: page 4—Erich Lessing/Art Resource, New York; page 5—
Mansell/Time Inc.; page 6—Scala/Art Resource, New York; pages 7, 10—Bibliothèque nationale de France; page 8 (right)—
Douglas Armand/Tony Stone Images; page 8 (lower left)—Trevor Wood/Tony Stone Images; pages 8 (upper left), 16, 18–19, 20, 29
(top), 30, 43—Hulton Getty/Tony Stone Images; page 9 (left)—Alinari/Art Resource, New York; page 9 (right)—Archive Photos;
page 11—copyright © The British Museum; page 17—Pepys Library, Magdalene College, Cambridge, United Kingdom; page 23
(top)—photograph by Eliot Elisofon, Eliot Elisofon Photographic Archives, National Museum of African Art; page 23 (bottom)—
John Elk III/Bruce Coleman Inc.; page 26 (lower right)—Wilberforce house, Kingston upon Hull City Museums, Art Gallery and
Archives, United Kingdom; pages 26 (top and lower left), 29 (bottom)—The Board of Trustees of the National Museums &
Galleries on Merseyside (Merseyside Maritime Museum), United Kingdom; page 31 (top)—Photographs and Prints Division,
Schomburg Center for Research in Black Culture, The New York Public Library, Astor, Lenox and Tilden Foundations; pages 31
(bottom), 39, 40–41, 42—New Haven Colony Historical Society, Connecticut; page 34—National Maritime Museum, London;
pages 36–37—by permission of the British Library.

Contents

Slavery in History

SLAVERY has been a fact of human life since early times. It was present in ancient Greece, Rome, Egypt, Mesopotamia, and throughout Africa. People in those areas of the world believed that slavery was part of the natural order.

There were two kinds of slaves in ancient times. The first were natives of a given society who fell into debt or committed a crime and were enslaved as punishment. As a rule, their enslavement was for a set period of years, after which they were freed.

The second kind of slaves were captives of war or victims of kidnapping or piracy. They could expect to remain slaves for the rest of their lives and to pass on their status to their children.

Treatment of slaves and their rights, if any, varied with the culture and the times. In some cultures, slaves could be imprisoned in place of their owners or buried with them when they died. In others, slaves could themselves own slaves.

Among the people of the ancient empires, the Romans practiced slavery to the greatest extent. At its height in the second century A.D., the Roman Empire

Egyptian slaves made up much of the labor force that built the pyramids. This fifteenth-century B.C. fresco from the tomb of Mennah shows an Egyptian foreman beating a slave.

Slaves attend their owner in a draper's shop in this second-century A.D. Roman relief.

stretched from England to North Africa. Providing food for Roman armies and developing lands they had conquered required cheap labor. For these purposes, the Romans used slaves, taken mostly from the peoples they had subjugated.

Later, in the middle of the seventh century A.D., crusading followers of the prophet Muhammad marched from Arabia to conquer Syria, Palestine, Egypt, Tunisia, Libya, and Morocco. These Muslims enslaved many of the people they conquered, for the same reasons as the Romans had.

The last major era of slavery in human history also had its roots in the spread of empires—in this case, the New World empires established by Portugal, Spain, the Netherlands, France, and England. When these Europeans began to colonize the Americas in the sixteenth century, they discovered rich natural resources. To mine America's ores and later work its vast agricultural plantations, they needed huge amounts of cheap labor. Colonists first enslaved the peoples they had conquered— the native Americans they called Indians. But as the supply of native Indian slaves diminished, they turned to Africa as a continual source of manpower.

Europe in 1492

WHEN Columbus made his first voyage to the Americas in 1492, he was sailing from a Europe just beginning to emerge from the Middle Ages. The level of everyday violence there was extremely high. In 1481, under the joint direction of King Ferdinand and Queen Isabella, the Spanish Inquisition began to discover and punish Jews, and later Muslims, suspected of only pretending to convert to Christianity while continuing to practice their original faiths. Soon, no Spanish converts were safe, and many were tortured and put to death. But elsewhere, life for ordinary Europeans was hard, too. Most were illiterate peasant laborers bound to the land—which was owned by a ruling class of monarchs, aristocrats, and church officials—as were their children and their children's children. Famine, plagues, and a high rate of infant mortality kept life expectancy short.

Nevertheless, changes were under way. A new middle class was rising, and cities such as Rome and Genoa in Italy and Lisbon in Portugal were filled with merchants, who traded in everything from textiles to weapons to jewelry. And the arts and sciences were flourishing.

(Above) A woman condemned by the Inquisition is led to the gallows in this mid-nineteenth-century painting by Eugenio Lucas.

Tailors, furriers, a barber, and a grocer are busy at work in this medieval French village scene.

7

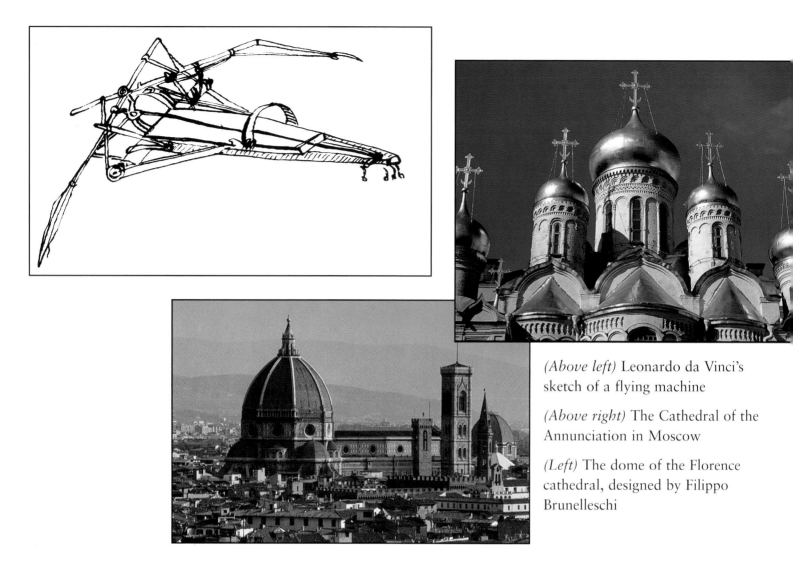

(Above left) Leonardo da Vinci's sketch of a flying machine

(Above right) The Cathedral of the Annunciation in Moscow

(Left) The dome of the Florence cathedral, designed by Filippo Brunelleschi

Art: In Italy, Leonardo da Vinci had already painted his magnificent *Adoration of the Magi* and was about to begin his famous *Last Supper*. Michelangelo Buonarroti was becoming known as a sculptor.

Architecture: The cathedral in Florence, Italy, had been completed in 1446, its dome a technological triumph. In Russia, Ivan the Great had hired the Italian architect Aristotle Fioravanti to build the Cathedral of the Annunciation, which was completed in 1489.

Mathematics: In 1489, the + (plus) and – (minus) signs came into use in mathematics for the first time.

Education: In Germany, Johann Gutenberg had invented movable type in the 1450s, and by 1492 printing presses were operating all over Europe. More people were thus able to learn to read and write.

Music and Dance: The first printed music appeared in Europe in 1465. In Italian royal courts, the dance form now known as ballet was first performed in 1490.

Science: In Italy, Leonardo da Vinci was designing a helicopter. In Germany, geographer Martin Behaim constructed the first terrestrial globe.

Exploration: Portuguese navigators had discovered the Gold Coast of West

(Above) Leonardo da Vinci's *Adoration of the Magi*

(Right) Johann Gutenberg, right, inspects a proof sheet in an engraving by O. Pelton.

Africa in 1470. In 1484, Diego Cam of Portugal found the mouth of the Congo River. Two years later, another Portuguese reached Angola.

Politics: By the end of the fifteenth century, European nation-states were emerging, with power centralized in strong monarchs. For the next four hundred years, the European states would be at war with one another almost constantly.

The European monarchs began to look for new sources of wealth outside their own borders and those of the continent itself. While the Portuguese concentrated on finding an eastern sea route to Asia, gradually working their way down the west coast of Africa and rounding the Cape of Good Hope in 1497, Spain looked for a more direct westerly route to the same destination. Christopher Columbus was financed by the king and queen of Spain when he set off on his voyage of discovery in 1492. His search unexpectedly brought him to the Americas, and within fifty years Spain and Portugal had overrun Central and South America, first plundering their precious metals such as gold and silver and then establishing large plantations for the production of sugar and tobacco. The European powers also built trading posts on the west coast of Africa, which eventually became launching points for the transport of millions of African slaves to the New World colonies.

Africa in 1492

I N 1492, Africa's population was about the same as Europe's—approximately fifty-five million people—and marked by a great diversity of cultures and economies. As in Europe, the majority of people were farmers, but the land they farmed was not owned by an elite class of aristocrats and church officials. In Africa, there was no such thing as private ownership of land. Instead, family and kinship groups owned the land in common.

Farm and village societies existed side by side with vast kingdoms and were dependent on them, as African kings, like those in Europe, helped to keep the peace in their region and encourage its economy. However, government in African empires was based on a system of obligation and customary law rather than of force, as in Europe, and violence as an everyday occurrence was rare.

(Above) Mali's emperor, Mansa Musa, is shown seated majestically on a throne in this map of West Africa drawn by Abraham Cresques in 1375.

Among the greatest of the African empires in 1492 was Mali. In the fifteenth century, it was one of the world's largest. Other great African empires of the time included Benin, Dahomey, and Kongo.

The major cities in these kingdoms were centers of commerce, craftsmanship, and learning. Bronze castings unearthed at the site of the ancient city-state of Ife, in the kingdom of Benin, reveal a technology more advanced than that in Europe during the same period. The city of Timbuktu, on the Middle Niger River, boasted the university of Sankor, where scholars from near and far studied and taught.

When the Portuguese arrived on the west coast of Africa in the late fourteenth century, they coveted African lands and riches. But the coastal African empires were much too strong to be conquered, and the Portuguese (and later other Europeans) had to be content with establishing trading posts. A flourishing, mutually beneficial exchange of goods developed. In addition to gold, the Europeans sought ivory, iron implements, palm oil, and textiles. As early as 1441, the Portuguese also sought slaves.

In 1441, Antam Goncalves, a Portuguese sailor, seized ten Africans near Cape Bojador. Although Goncalves kidnapped the Africans, this event is cited frequently as the beginning of the Atlantic slave trade. Since kidnapping could not be undertaken for long without incurring retribution from Africans, that method of obtaining slaves soon yielded to a formal trade. Portuguese traders exchanged horses, silks, and silver for slaves, whom they transported back to Portugal to work as domestic servants. Since slavery was common in Africa, rulers there saw no reason not to engage in this type of trade as well, and by 1448 there were one thousand African slaves in Portugal. In 1455, eighteen African slaves could be had in exchange for one horse and sold for a profit of 500 to 700 percent.

(Top) Bronze head, Benin, Nigeria

(Bottom) Bronze head, Ife, Nigeria

Slavery in Africa

SLAVERY was a traditional part of African life and was usually either a punishment for a crime or a result of war. African slaves were accorded different rights in different areas, but as a general rule they were treated like junior members of the community. Among the Ashanti, slaves were allowed to marry and own property, including slaves of their own. They could testify in court and even inherit their master's estate. Their children could marry the children of their masters. The sale of slaves outside the community was rare and, except for the trans–Saharan trade in slaves conducted with Arabs from the north, occurred only as a result of war.

With the beginning of the European trade in African slaves, however, the nature of slavery in Africa began to change. In 1481, the Portuguese built a fort at Elmina on the Gold Coast. From that base, they sailed down the coast, trading with local rulers for slaves. At the mouth of the Congo River, they encountered the ruler Nizinga Mvemba, who provided slaves to the Portuguese by leading military expeditions against the Mbundu tribe to the south and selling those he captured.

By providing guns and gunpowder, European slave traders encouraged such expeditions. In 1703, the Dutch West India Company supplied the state of Akwamu on the Gold Coast with one hundred soldiers and guns to wage war against their neighbors. Warfare for slaves introduced a level of violence previously unknown in African society. A slave ship captain wrote that "the far greater part of the wars in Africa, would cease, if the Europeans would cease to tempt them with goods for slaves."

After a time, the African chiefs were unable to control the slave trade within their borders. By 1526, Nizinga Mvemba, who by this time had converted to Christianity and taken the name Afonso I, wrote to the king of Portugal that the Portuguese "daily seize our subjects, sons of the land and sons of our noblemen and vassals and our relatives. . . . They grab them and cause them to be sold; and so great . . . is their corruption and licentiousness that our country is being utterly depopulated."

(Right) Fort Elmina

New World Slaves

THE need for slaves in the New World was growing rapidly. Spanish and Portuguese colonies in Mexico, Central and South America, and the Caribbean badly needed cheap labor to work their gold and silver mines and the rich sugarcane plantations they had established. First introduced to Europe from India via the Middle East in the Middle Ages, sugarcane was considered such a luxury that it was sold from druggists' shelves as a costly medicine. It was also the main ingredient in rum, the alcoholic drink of choice in Europe.

At first, the Spanish and Portuguese colonists employed local Indians on the sugarcane plantations. But the native peoples proved reluctant workers. Moreover, having no immunities to European diseases, they soon succumbed to such maladies as smallpox. It is not known how many Lucayan were living on Samana Cay in 1492 when Christopher Columbus landed on that island and named it San Salvador, but within forty years, not a single one was left. The Arawaks and Caribs of the West Indies also disappeared completely. In central Mexico, between 1518 and 1585, the Indian population was reduced, by slave trading among the islands of the Caribbean and by death from disease, from 6.3 million to 1.9 million.

Africans were not as susceptible to disease as the native Indians, they were available in abundance, and the profits to be made from the African slave trade were enormous. Although Spain and Portugal were the first to establish themselves in the African slave trade, it was not long before other nations of Europe were engaged in the trade of human beings as well. After the Dutch seized a sizable portion of northern Brazil in 1630, the Netherlands became a major player in the slave trade and, by the 1640s, had seized the Portuguese strongholds on the African coast. The French and the Danes also engaged in the slave trade to develop their holdings in the Caribbean.

Sir John Hawkins

The English did not take an active part in the slave trade until after 1650, but once they did, they came to dominate it in many areas. In fact, an Englishman, Sir John Hawkins, is regarded as the Father of the Slave Trade because it was his idea to profit by the trade on each leg of the journey.

The Spanish and Portuguese typically returned to their homelands with their cargoes of African slaves before shipping them to the New World. Hawkins sailed directly from Africa to the New World colonies. There he sold his human cargo for New World goods and then returned to England to sell those goods for a profit. The second leg of this triangular trade, the voyage from Africa to the New World, came to be called the Middle Passage.

Hawkins made his first slave-trading voyage in 1562, setting sail from England in October with three ships and a crew of one hundred. In the Sierra Leone area, Hawkins attacked Portuguese and Spanish ships and captured three hundred slaves. He then set sail for the Spanish colonies of the New World, where he sold his slave cargo and used his profits to purchase ginger, sugar, and hides. Hawkins was able to buy so much that he had to purchase two extra ships to carry it all back. Returning to England in September 1563, he sold the goods for a huge profit.

John Hawkins's personal flag, which flew from the masts of his ships, carried the image of a bound African. Indeed, the triangular trade established by Hawkins soon proved to be the basis for huge wealth in the British empire. By the eighteenth century, according to a British writer in 1745, the African slave trade was "the Great Pillar and Support" of British trade with America, and the British empire was "a magnificent superstructure of American commerce and [British] naval power on an African foundation." The same could have been said about the New World empires of Portugal, Spain, France, and Holland between 1500 and 1850.

(Above) Sir John Hawkins led several slaving voyages on the flagship *Jesus of Lubeck.*

The map below shows the basic routes of the transatlantic slave trade. In the first leg of the journey, ships sailed from Europe (blue routes) loaded with such goods as guns and textiles to trade for slaves in Africa. The second leg (red routes), known as the Middle Passage, brought slaves across the Atlantic to ports in the New World, where they were traded for sugar, cotton, grain, and other raw materials. The third leg of the journey brought the ships back to Europe, where the raw materials were exchanged for goods to trade with the Africans for slaves.

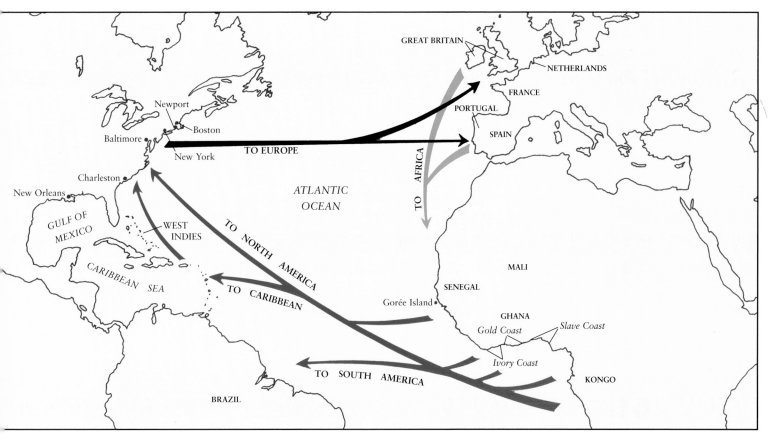

Capturing the Slaves

I N the early days of the trade, procuring slaves had been relatively easy for the Europeans. Coastal African chiefs readily traded slaves in exchange for European goods. In 1475, one Spanish expedition made an even greater profit than usual by dispensing with trade altogether and resorting to piracy. Three Spanish ships anchored at the mouth of the Gambia River, as if to trade honestly with the local people. But when the chief and some of his relatives went aboard to negotiate, they were seized and imprisoned instead. A landing party then rushed ashore and captured one hundred forty more people awaiting their chief's return.

But as New World development required more and more slaves and incidents such as the one just described made African chiefs along the coast more wary of the Europeans, acquiring slaves became more difficult. Europeans, unwilling to venture inland, turned to the burgeoning number of African slave merchants who, seeing the profits to be made, had turned from gold mining and trading in goods to capturing and exporting slaves.

Farmers and villagers might be snatched while working in their fields or walking on the road to town. Entire villages were raided. One trader reported that "an Abundance of little blacks of both sexes were stolen away by their neighbours, when found on roads in the wood."

Any West African, regardless of status, could be enslaved. In 1730, Ayuba Suleiman Diallo, who was about twenty-nine years old and a well-educated merchant in the Senegambian region of West Africa, was kidnapped and transported to Maryland.

A nineteenth-century slave raid in Central Africa

The March to the Coast

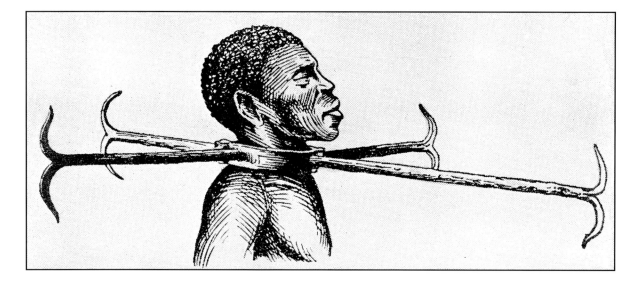

Slavers used neck rings to punish slaves and prevent their escape.

GROUPS of captives were bound together in coffles (from the Arabic *cafila*, meaning "caravan") and marched to coastal trading posts. Women and children were tied one behind the other with ropes. Men, who were more likely to try to escape, were secured more tightly. Sometimes two men were bound together with Y-shaped sticks around their necks, lashed together at midpoint. In other cases, their necks were encircled with iron collars and their wrists and ankles with iron cuffs. Then chains were passed through loops in the collars and cuffs so that each man's neck, wrists, and ankles were linked to those of the men behind and in front of him. By the 1700s, slaves were being captured as far as a thousand miles inland, and the march back to the coast might take sixty, seventy, or even eighty days. En route, the slaves might be forced to carry loads as heavy as sixty pounds for up to fifteen miles a day.

Slaves were constantly sold and resold in different markets in order to confuse them about the route home. In some instances, slaves were captured and recaptured by warring bands of slave kidnappers. Venture Smith, born in Dukandarra, Guinea, around 1729, was kidnapped by a neighboring tribe when he was only six years old. He later told of being marched four hundred miles and forced to carry on his head a large stone used for grinding corn, together with food and cooking utensils. Along the march route, the kidnappers added to their group of slaves. By the time they reached an area called Anamaboo, near the sea, their provisions and their strength were low. The people of Anamaboo saw their opportunity and attacked the kidnappers. According to Smith, they "took enemy, prisoners, flocks and all their effects. I was then taken a second time." Smith and the other recaptured slaves were transported to a European slave trading post near the coast.

Slave Holding Pens

UPON reaching the coastal area, the captives were taken to compounds where they were held for sale to slave-ship captains. In places where European traders had built large forts, there were underground dungeons, or "trunks," for holding the slaves. At Fort Elmina, built by the Portuguese on the coast of Ghana, stone-clad dungeons could hold up to a thousand slaves.

John Atkins, an eighteenth-century British naval surgeon, described the holding areas of a British trading base, Cape Coast Castle, as containing "large Vaults, with an iron Grate at the Surface to let in Light and Air on those poor Wretches, the Slaves who are chained and confined there till a Demand comes."

At the Niger Delta, holding pens were floating ship hulks, or *barracoons* (after the Spanish word *barraca,* or "warehouse"). In Angola, captives were usually held in open stockades, exposed to the blazing sun or the pouring rain except for some small areas covered by thatched roofs.

Once inside the holding pens, the slaves were stripped for examination and checked for evidence of disease or advanced age. Fifteen- to twenty-year-old males were the most sought after, and comprised about two-thirds of the slaves. The maximum age for a first-class slave was thirty-five. Merchants often ordered older men's heads shaved to conceal gray hair and their bodies rubbed with oil to give a healthy glow to the skin.

(Above right) Ruins of the House of Slaves, a slave-holding compound built about 1780 on Senegal's Gorée Island

(Below right) Cells inside the House of Slaves

Selecting Slaves for Purchase

WHEN enough slaves had been collected in the holding pen, a slave sale was held. The captives were herded out into an open marketplace and examined by slave-ship captains. Some captains preferred slaves of particular tribes. The French and Spanish considered the Fon from Dahomey and the Yoruba of western Nigeria especially hardworking.

Even more important than ethnic background was physical condition. The captains checked the captives for good teeth and flexible arms and legs, and had their own doctors examine them for signs of disease. The captains then negotiated a price for the slaves they wanted.

J. Taylor Wood, a midshipman on the United States brig *Porpoise,* described a group of slaves the *Porpoise* rescued from a Spanish slave ship in the mid-nineteenth century: "My charges were all of a deep black; from fifteen to twenty-five years of age, and, with a few exceptions, nude, unless copper or brass rings on their ankles or necklaces of cowries can be described as articles of dress. All were slashed, or had . . . scars . . . on their foreheads and cheeks; these marks were the distinguishing features of different tribes or families. . . . The figures of all were very good, straight, well developed. . . . Their hands were small, showing no evidences of work, only the cruel marks of shackles. These in some cases had worn deep furrows on their wrists or ankles."

Slave traders usually purchased the captives with European goods. In 1756, two slave ships out of the British coastal town of Newport recorded that African men were worth one hundred fifteen gallons of rum; women, fifty gallons. John Atkins recorded the price of a slave boy as seven fifty-pound kettles, five pieces of brawls (a blue-and-white-striped cloth manufactured in India), one piece of ramal (a soft leather), and one bar of iron. Venture Smith wrote in his memoirs that he was purchased by the ship's steward "for four gallons of rum, and a piece of calico, and called Venture, on account of his having purchased me with his own private venture. Thus I came by my name." Ottobah Cugoano of the Fanti tribe was sold at Cape Coast Castle for "one gun, one piece of cloth and a small quantity of lead."

Prices rose over time. In the late seventeenth century, British slave traders on the Guinea coast could buy slaves for about three English pounds each and sell them in the West Indies for sixteen or seventeen pounds. A century later, the price for slaves averaged twenty to twenty-five pounds.

Branding Slaves

I T was common practice to brand slaves with the mark of whoever had financed the expedition. Ship surgeon John Atkins reported that the slaves taken to the British trading base of Cape Coast Castle were branded with *DY* to indicate ownership by the Duke of York.

John Barbot, an agent for the French Royal African Company who made at least two voyages to the west coast of Africa, in 1678 and 1682, wrote that after the slaves found to be too old or diseased or otherwise considered defective were set aside, "each of the others, which have passed as good, is marked on the breast, with a red-hot iron, imprinting the mark of the French, English, or Dutch companies, that so each nation may distinguish their own, and to prevent their being chang'd by the natives for worse, as they are apt enough to do. In this particular, care is taken that the women, as tenderest, be not burnt too hard."

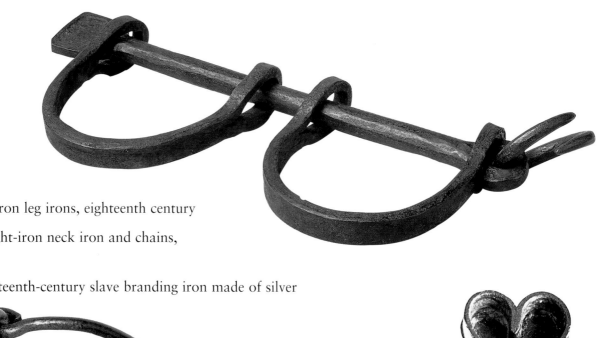

(Above) Wrought-iron leg irons, eighteenth century

(Below left) Wrought-iron neck iron and chains, eighteenth century

(Below right) Nineteenth-century slave branding iron made of silver

Leaving the African Shore

THE branded slaves were then returned to the slave pens, where they were fed bread and water until the sea was calm enough to send them aboard the ships lying at anchor off the coast. In January, February, and March, generally the months of calmest seas, the wait was only a day or so; but at other times the wait could be weeks.

When they learned that the cruel, pale-skinned strangers intended to load them aboard the ships and put them out to sea, the slaves were terrified. They had no idea what awaited them, and rumors flew. John Barbot reported that many believed the Europeans intended to eat them. Mungo Park, who explored the Niger River in the late 1700s, recalled hearing such rumors and trying to explain that after a journey across the sea, they would be put to work tilling the land. One of the slaves put his hand on the ground and asked whether there really was dry earth across the sea.

Ottobah Cugoano described being taken to a ship anchored offshore from Cape Coast Castle: "There was nothing to be heard but the rattling of chains, smacking of whips, and the groans and cries of our fellow-men. Some would not stir from the ground, when they were lashed and beat in the most horrible manner. . . . And when we found ourselves at last taken away, death was more preferable than life, and a plan was concerted amongst us that we might burn and blow up the ship and to perish altogether in the flames; but we were betrayed by one of our countrymen."

Chained together and loaded into long boats to be taken out to the slave ships at anchor, whole groups of slaves would jump together into the pounding surf. Believing that unimaginable horrors lay ahead, many desperately attempted this means of escape, even though, having grown up in the interior, they could not swim. They preferred death in the shark-infested waters to what they feared awaited them.

During the years of the African slave trade, the seas near slave-holding installations on the African coast became especially attractive to sharks, which recognized a good feeding ground when they found one. Sharks often followed slave ships across the Atlantic, waiting for people to jump or be thrown overboard.

(Right) Captains sometimes threw sick Africans overboard to prevent diseases from spreading.

(Below) "Armed Brig in the Mersey," a painting by John Jenkinson, about 1810, shows a typical slaving vessel.

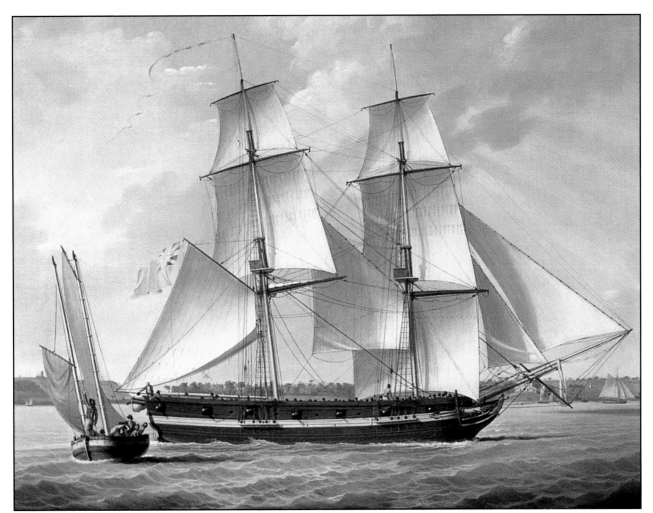

Conditions on Slave Ships

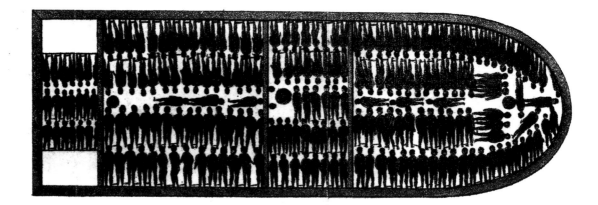

THE slave ships were known as "guineamen" or "slavers." In the early days of the slave trade, regular merchant ships were fitted out to carry human cargo. Later on, ships were especially built for the purpose.

The ships' cargo space was fitted with slave decks. The section for adult male slaves was located in the forepart of the lower deck. Amidships was the boy slaves' section, and behind this was the section for women and girls. Wooden platforms installed between the upper and lower decks were equipped with chains to secure the captives. The vertical spaces between them varied from ship to ship. Under the most humane conditions, the slaves could either sit up or lie down on the platforms. But greed often caused captains on slavers to disregard humane conditions. On some voyages of the *Brookes,* out of Liverpool, England, slaves were packed so closely together that it was impossible for them to lie down without resting their legs or other parts of their bodies on top of one another. Space for five men was not more than that of two modern single beds.

John Newton, an eighteenth-century British slave trader, described the slave hold on a hundred-ton ship that could carry between two hundred twenty and two hundred fifty people: The slaves, he said, lay below the deck "in two rows, one above the other, on each side of the ship, close to each other like books upon a shelf. . . . The poor creatures, thus cramped, are likewise in irons for the most part which makes it difficult for them to turn or move or attempt to rise or to lie down without hurting themselves. . . . Each morning perhaps more instances than one are found of the living and the dead fastened together."

(Above) This diagram of one deck of the hold of the slave ship *Brookes* shows the vessel filled to its intended capacity of 451. According to abolitionists, on some voyages the ship carried as many as 609 Africans.

Cross section of a slaving vessel, showing the crowded conditions on board

Slaves relieved themselves in slop buckets or tubs, which were emptied over the side of the ship. Dr. Alexander Falconbridge, who worked as a surgeon on several ships, wrote, "It often happens that those who are placed at a distance from the buckets, in endeavoring to get to them, tumble over their companions, in consequence of their being shackled. . . . In this situation, unable to proceed and prevented from going to the tubs . . . they ease themselves as they lie." Olaudah Equiano reported that children often fell into the tubs of human urine and feces. Shipboard conditions were so unsanitary that disease could spread unchecked. Dysentery, or diarrhea, was the most common ailment, and the most lethal killer. It was said that the stench of a slave ship could be smelled five miles away.

Slaves were often stowed sitting up or on their sides, wedged together like spoons.

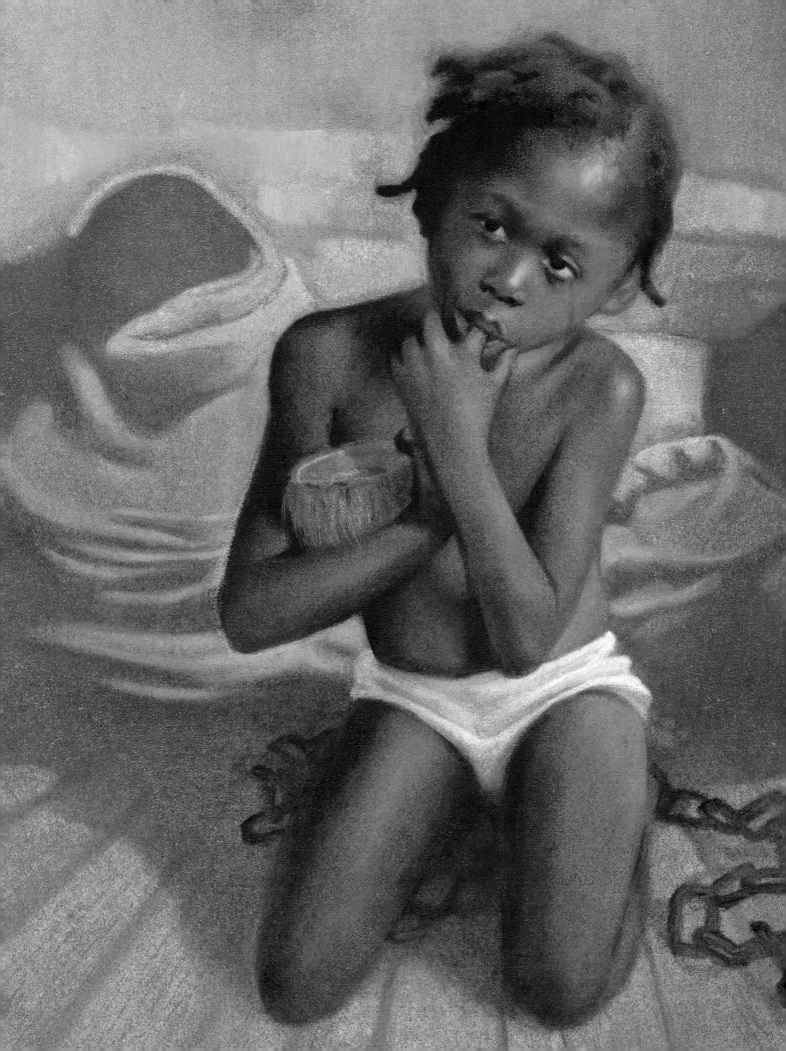

Feeding the Slaves

IN the time of the slave trade, the Atlantic crossing took an average of five weeks, but under adverse weather conditions it could take as long as three months. Supplies of drinking water and food—mostly a dried meat called hardtack and a dry bread called sea biscuit—usually ran low before the journey was over. Fresh food obtained in the African coastal ports was available at the beginning of the journey, but what was not eaten soon spoiled.

During the ocean passage, slaves were ushered up on deck in groups to be fed twice a day, once in the late morning and again in the late afternoon. A typical meal was porridge—one peckful for each ten slaves—followed by water. James Barbot, Jr., a sailor on the English slaver *Don Carlos*, wrote of conditions on a ship where care was taken to keep the slaves healthy: "We mess'd the slaves twice a day. . . . The first meal was of our large beans boil'd, with a certain quantity of Muscovy lard. . . . The other meal was of pease, or of Indian wheat . . . boiled with either lard, or suet, or grease. . . . I found they had much better stomachs for beans, and it is a proper fattening food for captives. . . . At each meal we allow'd every slave a full coconut shell of water, and from time to time a dram of brandy, to strengthen their stomachs." Other accounts of the slaves' daily ritual at sea state that, as the slaves were returned below decks, each was given a pint of water.

It was common for slaves aboard ship to attempt suicide by starving themselves. To combat the problem, some captains ordered the slaves beaten. Olaudah Equiano recalled, "I became so sick and low that I was not able to eat, nor had I the least desire to taste anything. I now wished for my last friend, death, to relieve me; but soon, to my grief, two of the white men offered me eatables, and on my refusing to eat, one of them held me fast by the hands and laid me across I think the windlass, and tied my feet while the other flogged me severely." When whipping didn't work, crew members scorched the slaves' mouths with hot coals. When all else failed, they resorted to a speculum oris, a specially designed mouth opener, containing dividers and a thumbscrew, that was hammered into the slave's mouth to keep it open. Food was then poured down the throat through a funnel.

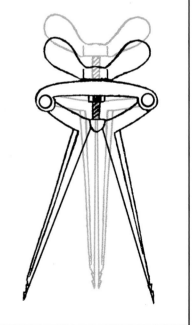

A speculum oris

Dancing the Slaves

WHEN the weather was good and conditions were peaceful, slaves were also allowed on deck to exercise. This was done for a very practical purpose: to keep the slaves as healthy as possible so they would be salable at journey's end. "Dancing the slaves" was a common practice. Sometimes a slave provided music for this exercise by beating on a drum or the bottom of a pot or strumming on an African stringed instrument that European observers variously called a banjo, banjar, bangelo, or bonjour. At other times, a member of the crew would play a bagpipe or fiddle. Slaving captains were known to advertise for sailors who could play a musical instrument, just for this purpose.

The slave-ship surgeon Dr. Alexander Falconbridge wrote in his 1788 book *An Account of the Slave Trade on the Coast of Africa,* "Exercise being deemed necessary for the preservation of their health, they are sometimes obliged to dance, when the weather will permit their coming on deck. If they go about it reluctantly, or do not move with agility, they are flogged; a person standing by them all the time with a cat-o'-nine-tails [a whip with nine leather straps] in his hand for that purpose. Their music, upon these occasions, consists of a drum. . . . The poor wretches are frequently compelled to sing also; but when they do so, their songs are generally, as may naturally be expected, melancholy lamentations of their exile from their native country."

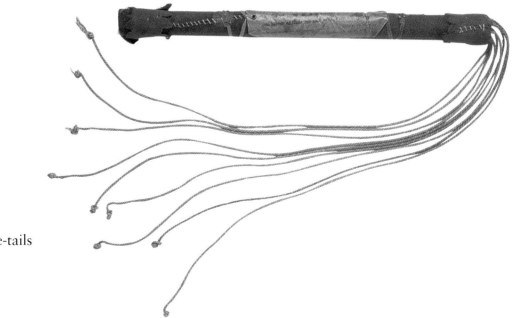

A cat-o'-nine-tails

Shipboard Mutinies

THE times slaves were allowed on deck presented some of the few occasions when they could organize revolts. Many slave rebellions occurred while the ships were still in sight of the African coast, when the slaves faced the immediate prospect of leaving their homeland and became most desperate. At least one hundred fifty slave mutinies at sea are recorded, but there is no way of knowing how many were attempted in the nearly four-hundred-year span of the African slave trade.

In 1682, the sailor James Barbot, Jr., witnessed a slave uprising aboard the English slaver *Don Carlos.* Armed with knives, which the unsuspecting captain had allowed them to have, and with pieces of iron they had torn off the forecastle door, a group of slaves fell on the crew, stabbing some and hurling them overboard. Other members of the crew fired upon the mutineers, killing and wounding many. Some slaves leaped overboard and drowned themselves. Altogether, some twenty-seven or twenty-eight slaves were lost. "The next day," according to Barbot, "we had them all again upon deck, where they unanimously declar'd, the Menbombe slaves had been the contrivers of the mutiny, and for an example we caused about thirty of the ringleaders to be very severely whipt. . . ."

In 1704, slaves revolted aboard the *Eagle,* anchored off Callabra. When brought on deck for their evening meal, the slaves, still shackled, attacked the chief mate and tried to throw a sentry overboard. Two slaves leaped overboard themselves. Their bodies, weighted down by the iron manacles, never came back to the surface.

In 1721, aboard the *Elizabeth,* a slave killed a sentry with a hatchet. He was caught and hanged from the foreyard arm. All the slaves on the surrounding ships were brought up on deck to witness the execution as a warning not to attempt a similar mutiny. To intimidate them further, the hanged man's body was cut down and his head severed and thrown into the sea. Some Africans believed that the spirit of a man whose body was so mutilated could not return to his homeland.

Insurrection on board a slave ship, from W. Fox's *Brief History . . .* , 1851

Also around 1721, a slave who had been nicknamed Captain Tomba enlisted the help of one male and one female slave to overpower the five sentries on guard duty one night. But as the plotters attacked the first sentry, two others were alerted by the noise and the revolt was foiled. Both Captain Tomba and his male confederate were young and strong and guaranteed to fetch a good price when sold. The captain decided not to kill them. Rather, he ordered them whipped and scarified with knife cuts. Three other male slaves had been in on the plot, although they had backed out at the last minute. Since they were in poor physical shape, the captain made an example of them. All three were killed. After the death of the first, the remaining two were forced to eat his liver and heart. Then they too were murdered. The woman was hoisted on a yardarm, whipped, and slashed with knives until she died.

Such attempts at mutiny were generally kept quiet, not only to prevent frightening ships' crews but also to avoid giving other slaves the notion that revolts were possible. But the captains of slave ships were certainly aware of previous mutinies and tried to prevent them. They mixed together slaves from different regions and tribes in a given cargo so there would be no common language to plan revolts. A smart captain never went among the slaves without armed sailors to act as guards. And when slaves did attempt to revolt, the captains usually ordered some killed, even though it meant losing part of their investment. Despite all these precautions, many slave mutinies did occur. And in several cases, the mutineers surprised the sailors, who thought the slaves had no knowledge of navigation, and managed to sail back home without the help of the crew.

The *Amistad* Revolt

THE most famous slave mutiny occurred late in the slave-trade era, in 1839. In the spring of that year, Cinque, the son of a Mende chief in Sierra Leone, was seized, sold to Portuguese slave traders, and shipped to Havana, Cuba. There, Cinque and about fifty other slaves were sold to two Spanish traders, who chartered the ship *Amistad* to journey to Puerto Principe in eastern Cuba.

Not long after the *Amistad*'s departure from Havana, Cinque and his compatriots seized the weapons of their sleeping guards and killed the ship's captain and cook. Two crewmen escaped in longboats. Cinque ordered the two Spanish traders to sail the ship back to Africa.

(Above) This shipboard scene is one in a series of murals, created by Hale Woodruff circa 1940, that tell the *Amistad* story.

The slave traders had no intention of doing so, and instead, at night when the Africans could not tell direction by the sun, they headed north and west, arriving some two months later off the coast of Long Island. Taken to Connecticut, the slaves were imprisoned while the United States tried to figure out what to do with them.

The Spanish slave traders insisted that the slaves be returned to them. But the United States had outlawed the importing of slaves in 1808, though it still went on in some states. Many Americans felt the Africans should be allowed to go free, arguing that they had been illegally kidnapped and that, in revolting and killing the

One of the Spanish traders points an accusing finger at Cinque in the courtroom scene from Woodruff's murals.

captain and cook, they had merely exercised their right to regain their freedom. Cinque testified on behalf of himself and his fellow Africans in the New Haven, Connecticut, courtroom, and so impressed his listeners that the court decided in their favor. The Spanish slave traders appealed the ruling to the United States Supreme Court.

Former president John Quincy Adams, in his early seventies and in poor health, agreed to represent the Africans. He argued successfully on behalf of Cinque and the other Africans, and the Supreme Court ordered the slaves freed. They returned to Sierra Leone in 1842.

More common than mutiny, however, was rebellion through suicide. Since many Africans believed that in death they would return to their own country, they considered it preferable to journeying to an unknown fate. Slaves threw themselves overboard, slit their own throats, hanged themselves, or attempted to starve themselves. The Ibo from eastern Nigeria were said to be the most likely to commit suicide.

Other slaves died for no apparent reason. Slave-ship doctors called the condition "fixed melancholy," a sadness so great that it ended in death. Many more died of diseases, most commonly of dysentery. Smallpox, too, was common, though not necessarily fatal.

It is estimated that, in the late 1600s, at least one of every four slaves died while crossing the Atlantic. In the 1700s, the shipboard death rate was lower (about one in eight), but one of every four survivors died within a few months of arriving in the New World. Historians have estimated that, at the height of the slave trade, about forty thousand Africans died each year.

Abolitionist Nathaniel Jocelyn painted this watercolor portrait of Cinque, leader of the *Amistad* revolt, while the Africans' case was moving through the courts.

The Journey Ends

Prospective buyers inspect a woman and child.

For those who survived, any relief they might have felt at being freed from their long and painful shipboard confinement was soon replaced by new terrors. John Newton, the English slave trader, wrote, "Yet, perhaps, they would wish to spend the remainder of their days on ship-board, could they know, beforehand, the nature of the servitude which awaits them on shore; and that the dreadful hardships and sufferings they have already endured, would to the most of them, only terminate in excessive toil, hunger, and the excruciating tortures of the cart-whip, inflicted at the caprice of an unfeeling overseer, proud of the power allowed him of punishing whom, and when, and how he pleases."

What awaited the Africans in the Americas was almost surely a life of drudgery and sorrow, of being worked like animals and of enjoying no more rights than animals. Remarkably, their strong sense of hope and self-worth, which helped them survive the Middle Passage, continued to gird them in their new lives. As they constructed towns, dug mines, cleared fields, and harvested crops in the New World, they helped build a new culture with their music and dance, their humor, and their skills in such areas as agriculture, metalworking, carpentry, and medicine. And as the passage of time caused the memory of Africa to dim, they made the New World their home.

Milestones in the History of Slavery

Between 1441, when Portuguese sailor Antam Goncalves seized ten Africans near Cape Bojador on the west coast of the continent, to 1807, when Britain abolished the slave trade, and 1808, when the United States outlawed any further importation of slaves, an estimated twelve million Africans were forced from their homeland and shipped to the New World as slaves. The following time line includes not only milestones in the Atlantic slave trade itself but also significant events in the lives of Africans in the New World during this more than three-hundred-sixty-year period.

1441 The first cargo of African slaves arrives at Lisbon with Antam Goncalves.

1448 By this time, about one thousand African slaves have been carried to Portugal from the Barbary Coast and Guinea.

1455 Eighteen African slaves can now be purchased in exchange for one horse.

1481 The Portuguese build a fort at Elmina on the Gold Coast as a base for their slave trade.

1485 São Tomé, an island two hundred miles off the African coast, becomes a slave marshaling area.

1492 African servants, slaves, and explorers come to the New World with the first Spanish and French explorers.

1501 The Spanish crown officially approves the use of African slaves in the New World.

1502 Portuguese land the first cargo of slaves in the New World.

1513 Spanish explorer Vasco Núñez de Balboa lands in South America and finds a community of black people already living there, suggesting that Africans "discovered" America before Columbus.

1517 To encourage immigration to the New World, Bishop Bartolomé de Las Casas petitions the Spanish crown to allow each Spanish settler to import twelve Africans.

1519 Three hundred Africans help Hernando Cortés defeat the Aztecs.

1526 Afonso I, chief of the Kongo, writes to the king of Portugal that the Portuguese trade in slaves is "depopulating" his country.

1528 Estevanico, the most important African explorer of America, arrives in Tampa Bay. He will become the first non–Native American to explore present-day Arizona and New Mexico.

There are now nearly ten thousand Africans in the New World. Although some have come as free people and some as indentured servants, most are enslaved.

1538 Escaped slaves set up the Gracia Real de Santa Teresa de Mose settlement in the area of present-day Florida, the first black settlement in North America.

1562 John Hawkins's first slaving expedition

1600 There are now about nine hundred thousand African slaves in Latin America.

1619 Twenty Africans, including three women, arrive in Jamestown, Virginia, on a Dutch ship and are sold not as slaves but as indentured servants. (Indentured servants worked as servants for a set term, usually seven years.)

1620 The *Mayflower* lands at Plymouth, Massachusetts.

1621 The Dutch West India Company is chartered, bringing Dutch merchants into the Atlantic slave trade.

1623 William Tucker is born in Jamestown, the first black child born in the English colonies.

1624 Samuel Maverick, New England's first slaveholder, arrives with two African slaves.

The Dutch begin to import African slaves to serve on Hudson Valley farms in present-day New York.

France enters the Atlantic slave trade.

1634 The first African slaves are imported to Maryland and Massachusetts.

1639 New England enters the slave trade when Captain William Pierce sails to the West Indies and exchanges enslaved Native Americans for Africans.

1641 A black former indentured servant, Mathias De Sousa, is elected to serve in the Maryland General Assembly.

Virginia passes a fugitive slave law punishing those who assist runaway slaves.

Massachusetts becomes the first colony to legally recognize the institution of slavery.

Eleven African indentured servants are awarded their freedom and a piece of land in what is now Greenwich Village in New York City.

1645 First known record of African slaves in New Hampshire

1649 There are now about three hundred African slaves in Virginia.

1651 Anthony Johnson, one of the twenty indentured Africans to arrive in Jamestown in 1619, launches an independent black community in Virginia, which at its height includes twelve black homesteads.

1652 Rhode Island enacts the first law against slavery in North America, limiting slavery to ten years.

1659 When the slave ship *St. Jan* reaches the West Indies on September 24, one hundred ten of the slaves aboard had died and the rest were in disastrous condition from want of food and sickness. Of the entire cargo, only ninety slaves were saved.

1660s Virginia (1661), Maryland (1663), New York (1664), and New Jersey (1664) legally recognize the institution of slavery.

1663 Carolina settlers are offered twenty acres for every male African slave and ten acres for every female brought into the colony.

1670 King Louis XIV of France notes: "There is nothing which contributes more to the development of the colonies and the cultivation of their soil than the laborious toil of the Negroes."

1671 There are now about two thousand African slaves in Virginia.

1672 The English form the Royal African Company.

1675 There are now about one hundred thousand slaves in the West Indies and five thousand in the North American colonies.

1677 Fifty-five African men, women, and children die aboard the *Arthur* before the ship even leaves for the New World.

1682 Slave uprising aboard the English slave ship *Don Carlos*

1700 There are now about twenty-eight thousand African slaves in the English North American colonies, twenty-three thousand of them in the South.

1703 The Dutch West India Company supplies the state of Akwamu on the Gold Coast with one hundred soldiers and guns to wage war against their neighbors to obtain slaves.

1704 Slaves revolt aboard the *Eagle,* anchored off Callabra.

1708 Black slaves outnumber whites in the Carolinas for the first time.

In a slave revolt in what is now New York City, nine whites are killed and twenty-one slaves are executed.

1720 Several slaves are burned alive and others are banished after they are implicated in a revolt near Charleston, South Carolina.

1721 In a slave rebellion aboard the *Elizabeth,* a slave kills a sentry with a hatchet and is hung from the foreyard arm. Slaves on the *Elizabeth* and surrounding ships are all brought on deck to witness the execution. To further intimidate the slaves, the head is cut off and thrown into the sea.

A slave nicknamed Captain Tomba initiates a slave-ship revolt, but it fails.

1730 Ninety-six Africans aboard the *Little George* wrest control of the ship from the crew. Despite their inexperience at navigation, they successfully pilot the ship back to Africa, where they escape.

1737 When the *Prince of Orange* arrives in Jamaica, at least one hundred Africans leap overboard to their deaths.

1739 About twelve slaves revolt at Stono, South Carolina. Marching southward toward freedom in Spanish Florida, the group swells to more than seventy-five slaves but is defeated about ten miles south of Stono.

1750 There are now about 236,000 African slaves in the English colonies, more than 206,000 of them living south of Pennsylvania.

1753 Benjamin Banneker (1731–1806), a freeborn Negro from Maryland, constructs the first striking clock with all parts made in America. It keeps perfect time for forty years.

1755 There are now about 240,000 African slaves and 90,000 whites in the West Indian islands.

1756 Male African slaves can now be purchased for one hundred fifteen gallons of rum, females for fifty gallons.

1769 Thomas Jefferson unsuccessfully presses the Virginia House of Burgesses for a bill to emancipate slaves.

1770 Crispus Attucks (b. 1723?), a runaway slave and seaman, is the first American killed by British soldiers in the Boston Massacre, March 5.

1773 Phillis Wheatley's *Poems on Various Subjects, Religious and Moral* is published, the first book written by a black in North America and the second by an American woman.

The first abolitionist society in the United States is organized in Philadelphia.

On November 7, Lord Dunmore, the deposed royal governor of Virginia, promises freedom to slaves who join the British army. On November 12, George Washington issues an order forbidding blacks from enlisting in the Continental Army. On December 12, alarmed by the impact of the Dunmore proclamation, Washington reverses himself and authorizes the enlistment of blacks.

At least one hundred thousand slaves run away from their masters during the Revolutionary War.

1776 The Declaration of Independence is adopted on July 4. A section denouncing the slave trade has been deleted.

1777 Vermont becomes the first colony to abolish slavery.

1778 By now, more than three thousand slaves have fought in the Revolutionary War.

1780 Pennsylvania passes a gradual emancipation law.

1780s Slavery is abolished in Massachusetts (1783), New Hampshire (1783), Connecticut (1784), and Rhode Island (1784).

1781 As the slave ship *Zong* nears Jamaica, more than sixty slaves and seven crew members have died from disease, and only two hundred gallons of water remain for the three hundred ninety persons still on board. Over the course of a few weeks in November and December, two hundred one sick slaves are thrown into the sea in order to collect the insurance, despite the fact that on December 1 rain replenishes the water supply.

1783 The Revolutionary War ends. Approximately ten thousand blacks have served in the Continental Army.

1786 Importation of new slaves ends in all states but South Carolina and Georgia.

1787 The Continental Congress prohibits slavery in the Northwest Territory.

The U.S. Constitution is approved with three clauses protecting slavery.

1790 There are now about 757,208 blacks in the United States, 19.3 percent of the total population (3,929,214); 59,557 are free.

1791 The Haitian Revolution begins on August 22 (ends on January 1, 1804). This is the only rebellion to liberate an entire slave population.

1792 Denmark abolishes its slave trade, effective 1793.

1793 The cotton gin, a machine that separates cotton fiber from its seed, is invented. This will lead to increased cotton cultivation in the Southern states, and to greater demand for slaves.

Congress passes the Fugitive Slave Act, which makes it a criminal offense to harbor a fugitive slave or prevent his arrest.

1799 New York passes a gradual emancipation law.

1800 There are now 1,002,037 blacks in the United States, 18.9 percent of the total population (5,308,483).

The price of a prime field slave is now about two hundred dollars.

1803 South Carolina opens an African slave trade with Latin America.

1804 New Jersey abolishes slavery.

1807 Britain abolishes its slave trade, effective May 1, 1807.

Two boatloads of enslaved Africans arriving in Charleston, South Carolina, starve themselves to death rather than submit to slavery.

1808 The United States outlaws the importing of slaves, effective January 1, 1808; from 1808 until 1860, however, approximately 250,000 slaves will be illegally imported.

There are now one million enslaved Africans in the United States.

Bibliography

Churchill, Awnsham and John, eds. *Collection of Voyages and Travels*. London: H. Lintot, 1732.

Conneau, Theophile. *Adventures of an African Slaver*. New York: Dover, 1969.

Davidson, Basil. *The African Slave Trade*. Boston: Little, Brown, 1980.

Equiano, Olaudah. *The Life and Adventures of Olaudah Equiano, or Gustavus Vassa, the African*. New York: Samuel Wood & Sons, 1829.

Everett, Susanne. *History of Slavery*. Secaucus, N.J.: Chartwell Books, 1994.

Falconbridge, Alexander. *An Account of the Slave Trade on the Coast of Africa*. London: J. Phillips, 1788.

Feelings, Tom. *The Middle Passage: White Ships, Black Cargo*. New York: Dial, 1995.

Inikori, J. E., ed. *Forced Migration: The Impact of the Export Slave Trade on African Societies*. London: Hutchinson, 1982.

Inikori, Joseph, and Stanley L. Engerman, eds. *The Atlantic Slave Trade*. Durham, N.C.: Duke University Press, 1992.

Kay, George F. *The Shameful Trade*. London: Muller, 1967.

Martin, Bernard, and Mark Spurrell, eds. *The Journal of a Slave Trader (John Newton) 1750–1754*. London: Epworth, 1962.

The Martin Luther King, Jr., 1995 Memorial Anthology. InterGo Communications, Inc., Project Gutenberg Association at Illinois Benedictine College, 1996.

Palmie, Stephan. *Slave Cultures and the Cultures of Slavery*. Knoxville: University of Tennessee Press, 1995.

Smith, Venture. *A Narrative of the Life and Adventures of Venture, A Native of Africa*. Middletown, Conn.: J. S. Stewart, 1897.

Tibbles, Anthony, ed. *Transatlantic Slavery: Against Human Dignity*. London: HMSO, 1994.

ESPECIALLY FOR YOUNG PEOPLE

Mann, Kenny. *Oyo, Benin, Ashanti: The Guinea Coast*. Parsippany, N.J.: Dillon, 1996.

Milsome, John R. *Olaudah Equiano: The Slave Who Helped to End the Slave Trade*. New York: Harlow, Longmans, 1975.

Nardo, Don. *Braving the New World, 1619–1784*. New York: Chelsea House, 1995.

Ofosu-Appiah, L. H. *People in Bondage: African Slavery in the Fifteenth Century*. Minneapolis, Minn.: Runestone, 1993.

Palmer, Colin A. *The First Passage: Blacks in the Americas, 1502–1617*. New York: Oxford University Press, 1995.

Steme, Emma Gelders. *The Slave Ship*. New York: Scholastic, 1975.

Zagoren, Ruby. *Venture for Freedom: The True Story of an African Yankee*. Cleveland, Ohio: World Publishing Co., 1969.

Index